# Atlas Of Human Anatomy Just For Kids

Speedy Publishing LLC
40 E. Main St. #1156
Newark, DE 19711

www.speedypublishing.com


9781681275536
First Printed January 8, 2015



speedypublishing

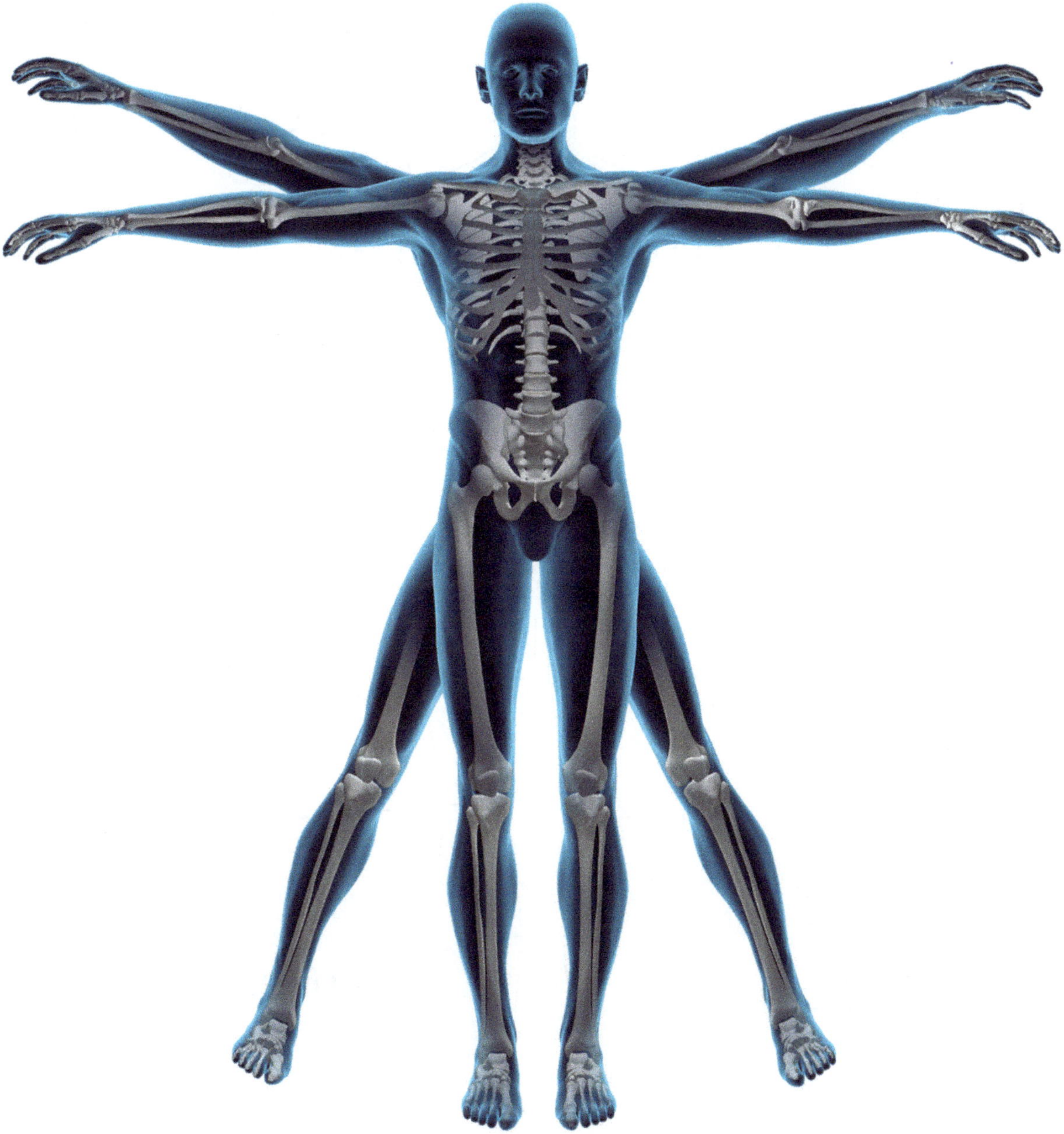

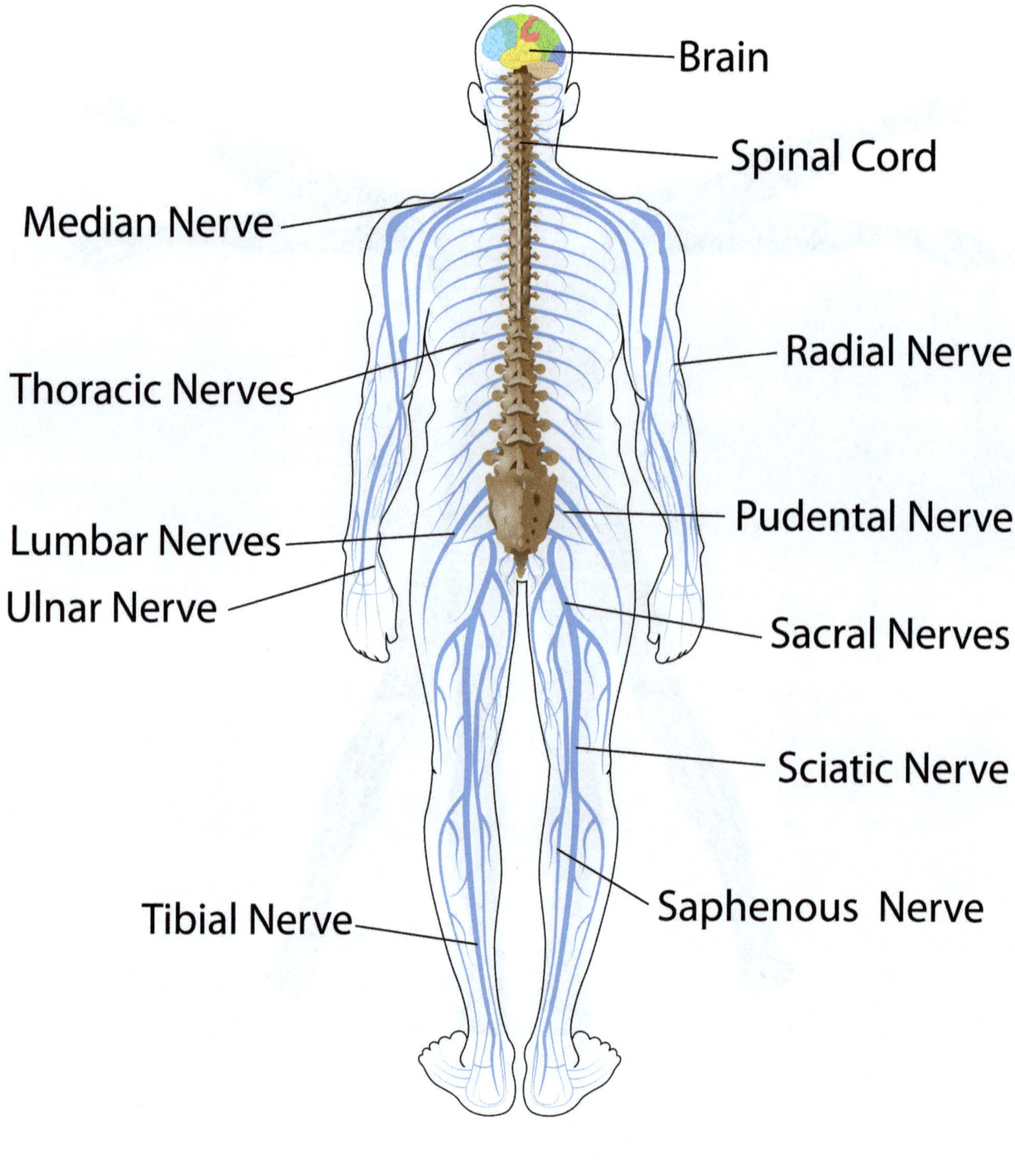
Brain
Spinal Cord
Median Nerve
Radial Nerve
Thoracic Nerves
Pudental Nerve
Lumbar Nerves
Ulnar Nerve
Sacral Nerves
Sciatic Nerve
Saphenous Nerve
Tibial Nerve

# Nervous System

The nervous system consists of the brain, spinal cord, sensory organs, and all of the nerves that connect these organs with the rest of the body. Together, these organs are responsible for the control of the body and communication among its parts. The brain and spinal cord form the control center known as the central nervous system (CNS), where information is evaluated and decisions made.

Neurons, also known as nerve cells, communicate within the body by transmitting electrochemical signals. Neurons look quite different from other cells in the body due to the many long cellular processes that extend from their central cell body. There are 3 basic classes of neurons: afferent neurons, efferent neurons, and interneurons.

# Types of Neurons

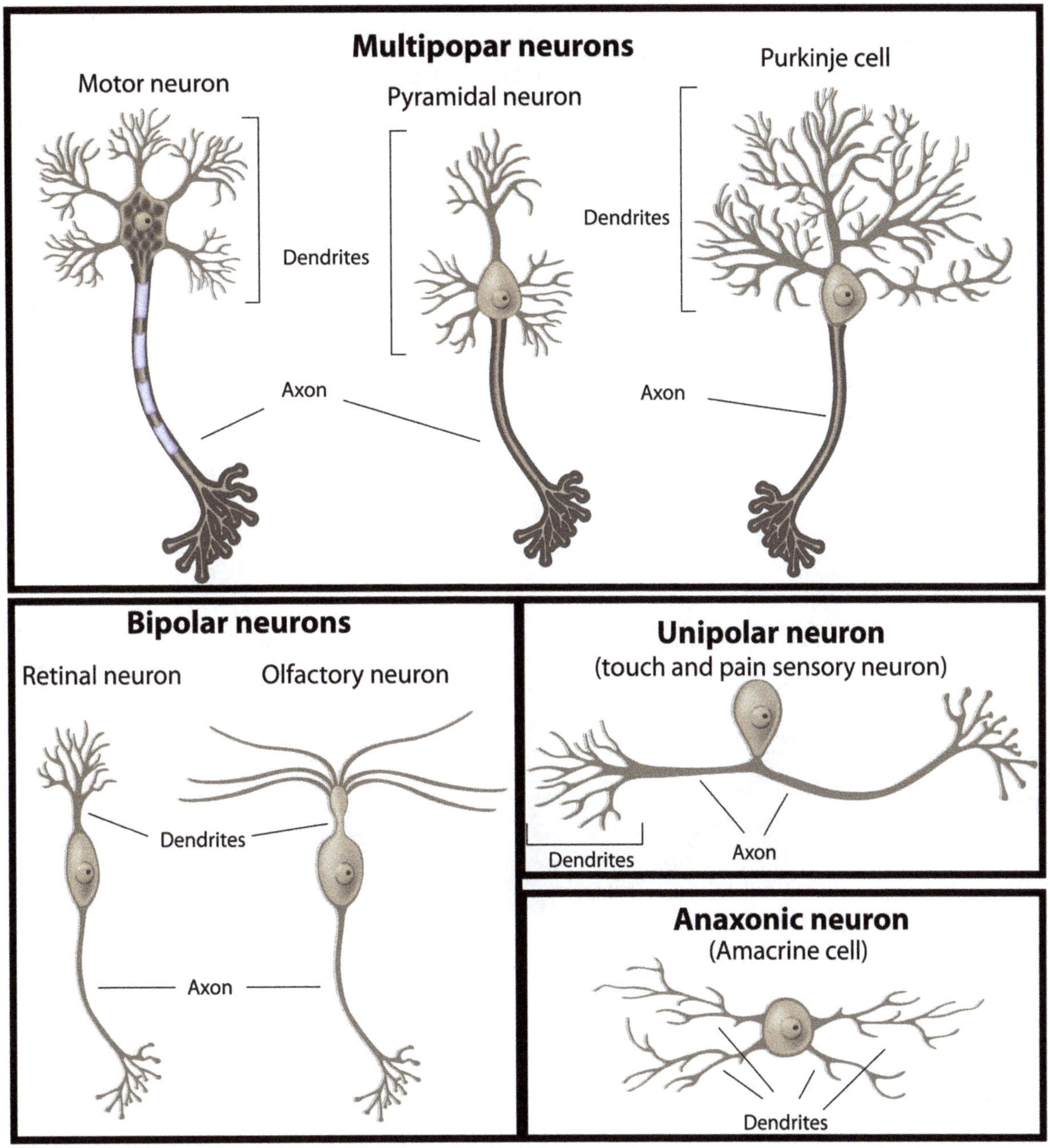

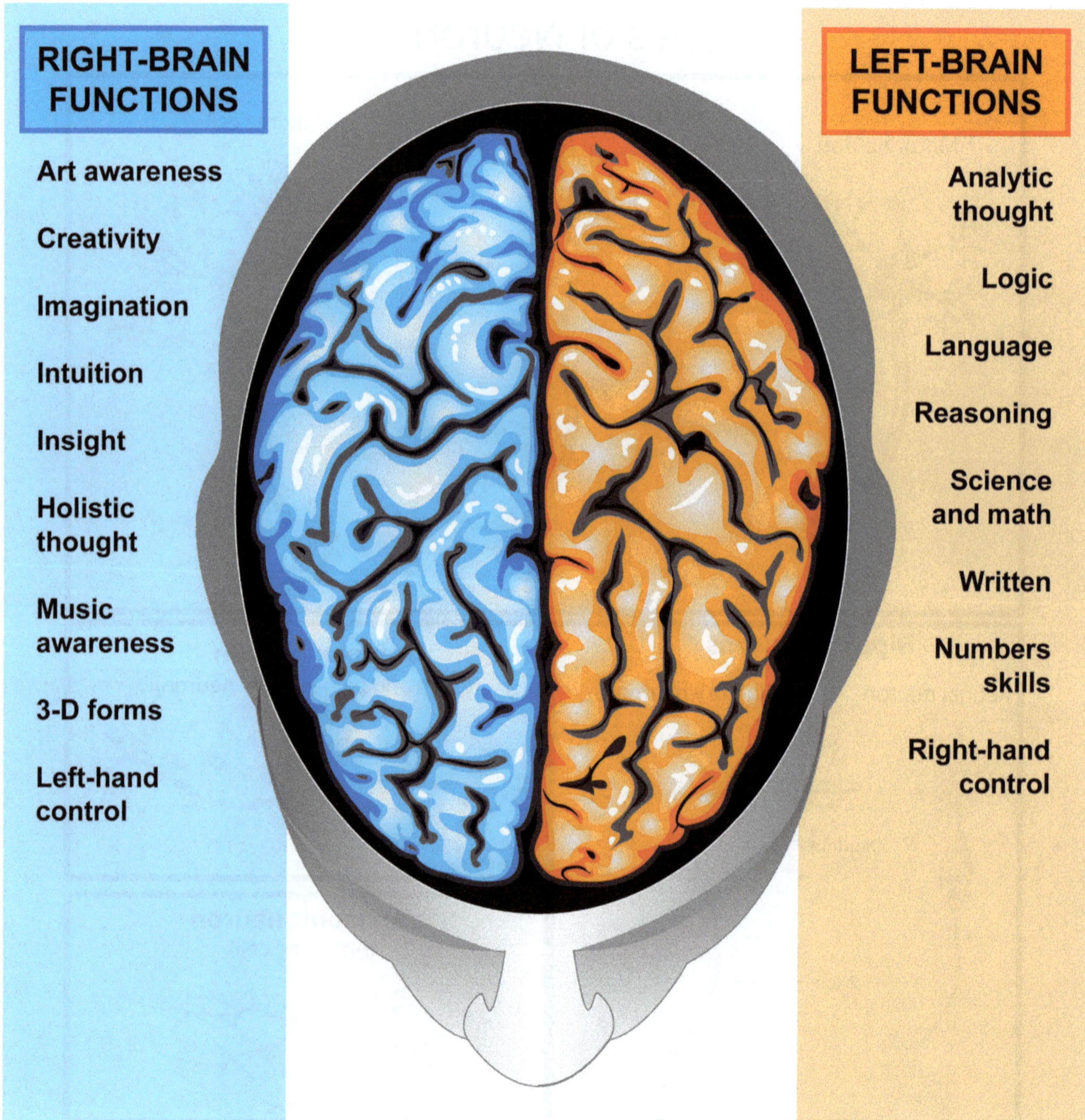
RIGHT-BRAIN FUNCTIONS
Art awareness
Creativity
Imagination
Intuition
Insight
Holistic thought
Music awareness
3-D forms
Left-hand control
LEFT-BRAIN FUNCTIONS
Analytic thought
Logic
Language
Reasoning
Science and math
Written
Numbers skills
Right-hand control

**The brain, the seat of higher mental functions such as consciousness, memory, planning, and voluntary actions, also controls lower body functions such as the maintenance of respiration, heart rate, blood pressure, and digestion.**

# Circulatory System

Responsible for transporting oxygen, nutrients, hormones, and cellular waste products throughout the body, the cardiovascular system is powered by the body's hardest-working organ — the heart, which is only about the size of a closed fist. Even at rest, the average heart easily pumps over 5 liters of blood throughout the body every minute.

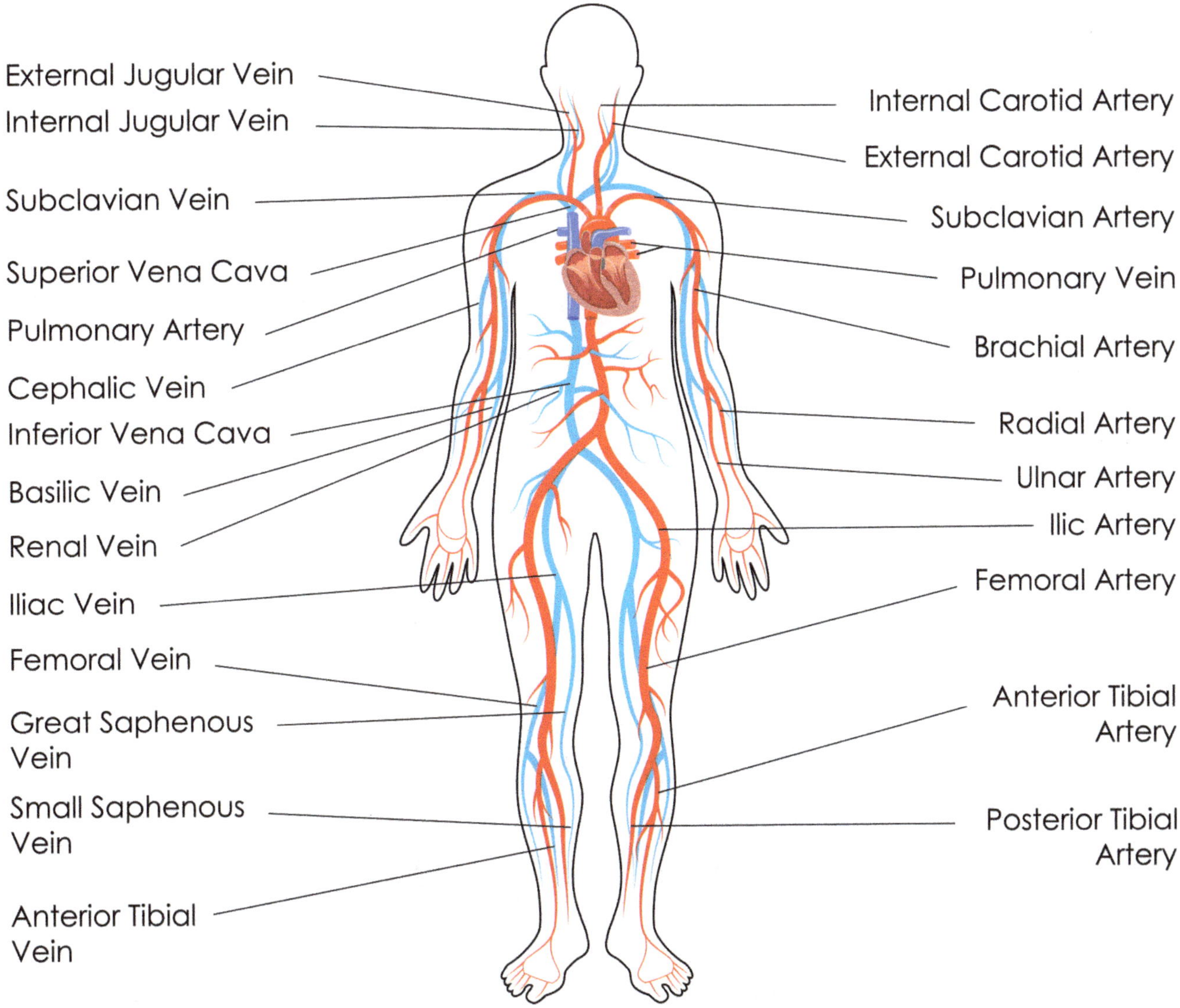


# CIRCULATORY SYSTEM

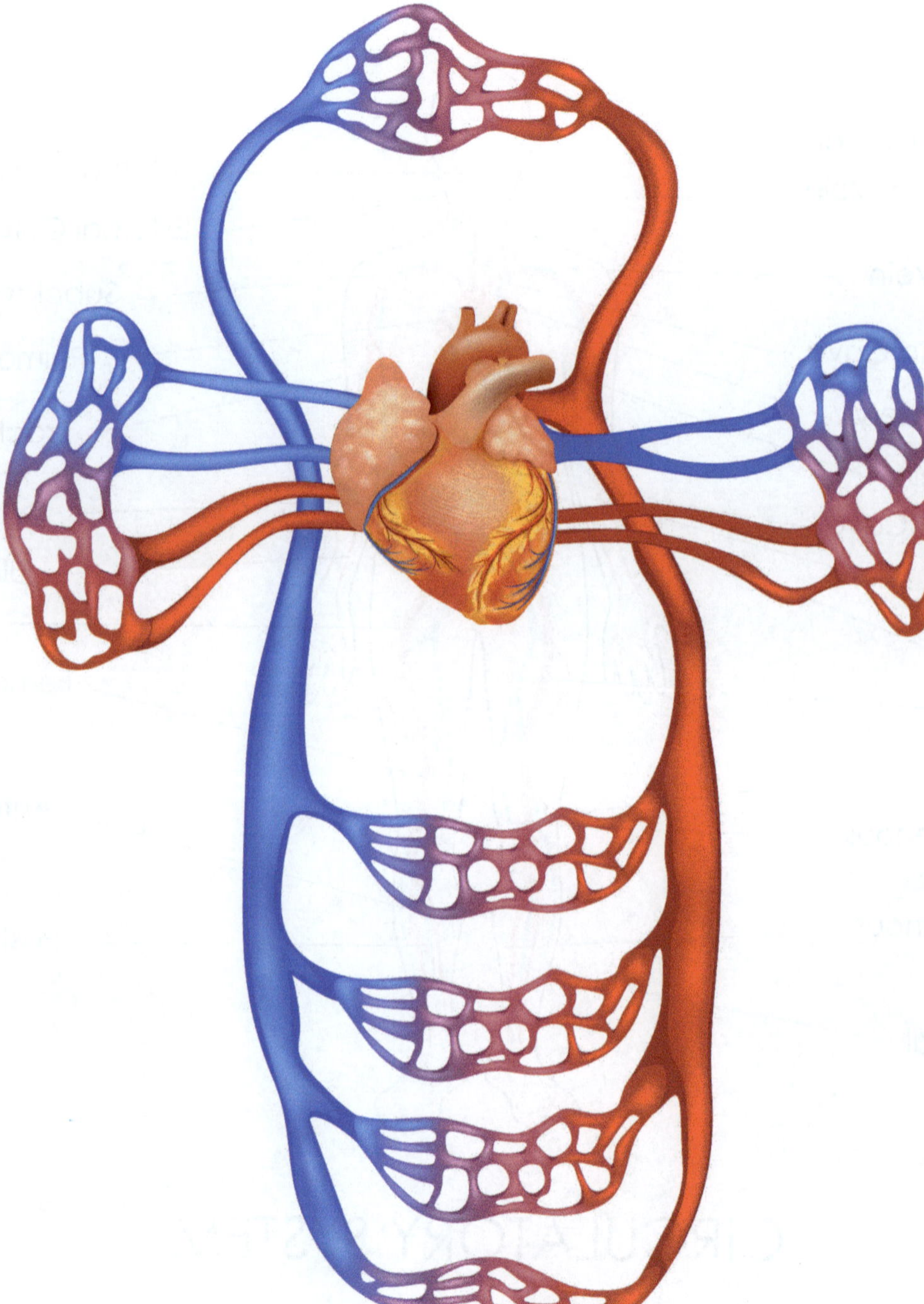

**Blood vessels are the body's highways that allow blood to flow quickly and efficiently from the heart to every region of the body and back again. The size of blood vessels corresponds with the amount of blood that passes through the vessel. All blood vessels contain a hollow area called the lumen through which blood is able to flow.**

The heart is a muscular pumping organ located medial to the lungs along the body's midline in the thoracic region. The bottom tip of the heart, known as its apex, is turned to the left, so that about 2/3 of the heart is located on the body's left side with the other 1/3 on right. The top of the heart, known as the heart's base, connects to the great blood vessels of the body: the aorta, vena cava, pulmonary trunk, and pulmonary veins.

# Anatomy of the Human Heart

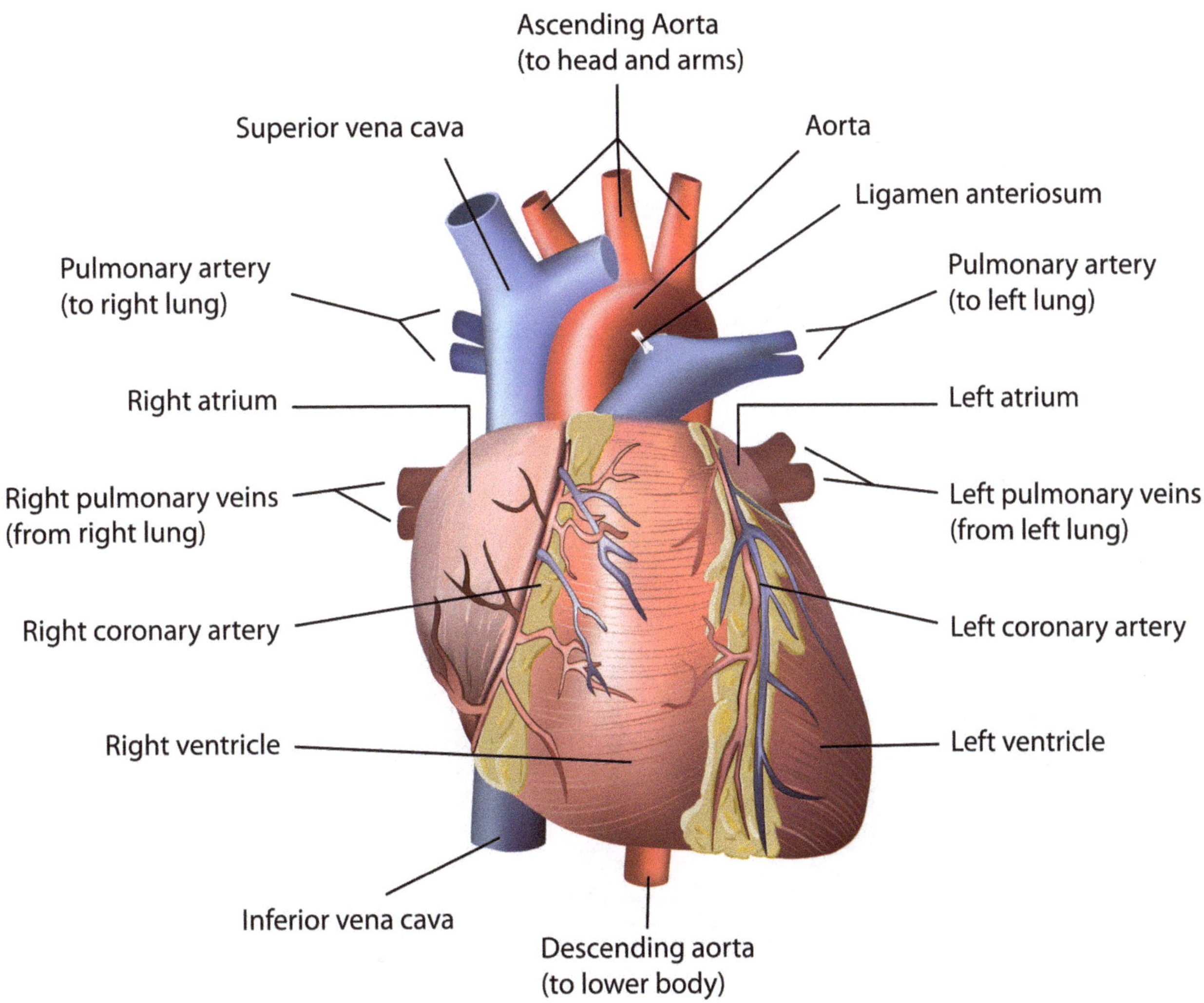

# The Respiratory System

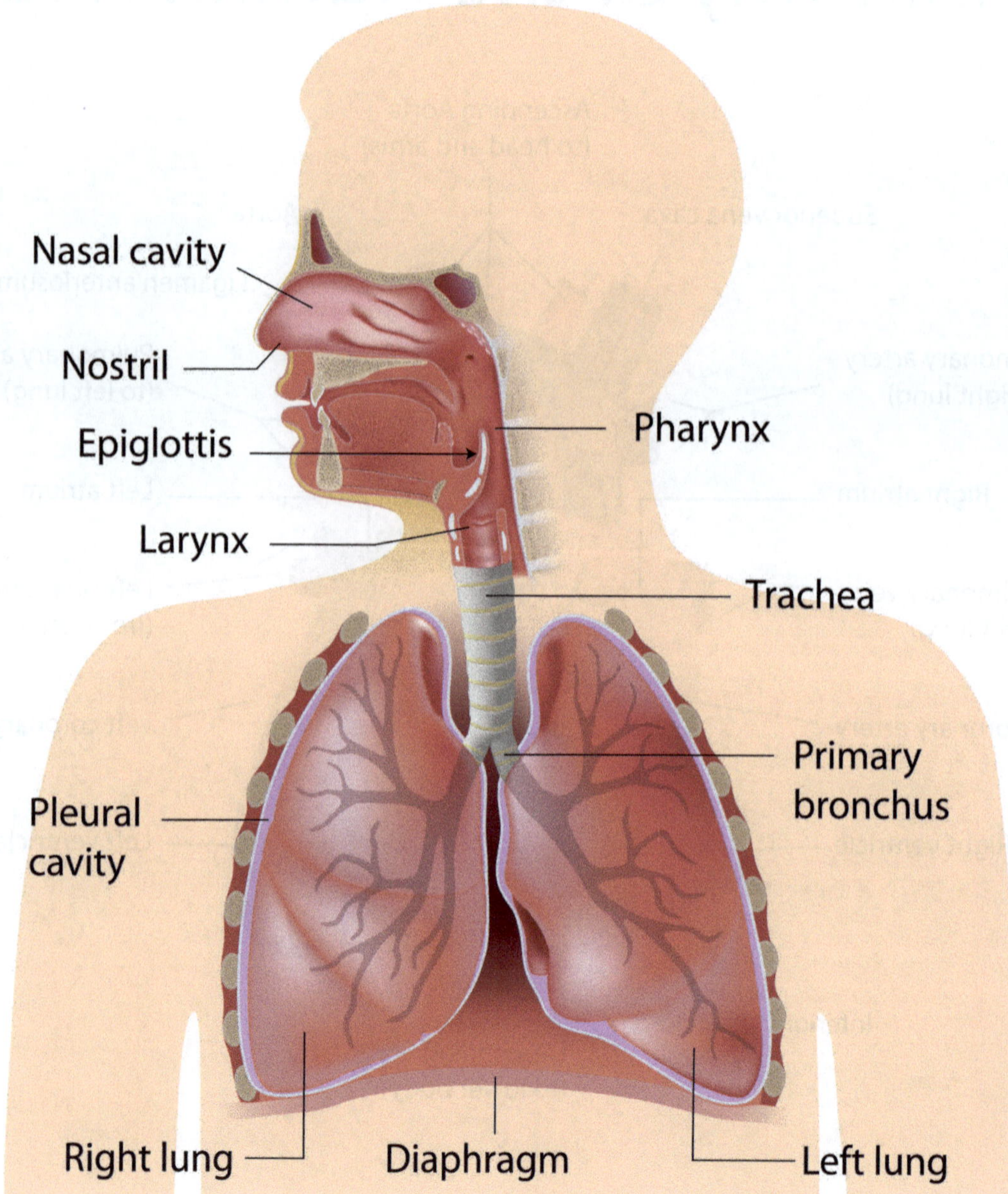

# Respiratory System

The respiratory system provides oxygen to the body's cells while removing carbon dioxide, a waste product that can be lethal if allowed to accumulate. There are 3 major parts of the respiratory system: the airway, the lungs, and the muscles of respiration. The airway, which includes the nose, mouth, pharynx, larynx, trachea, bronchi, and bronchioles, carries air between the lungs and the body's exterior.

The larynx, also known as the voice box, is a short section of the airway that connects the laryngopharynx and the trachea. The larynx is located in the anterior portion of the neck, just inferior to the hyoid bone and superior to the trachea.

# The Larynx

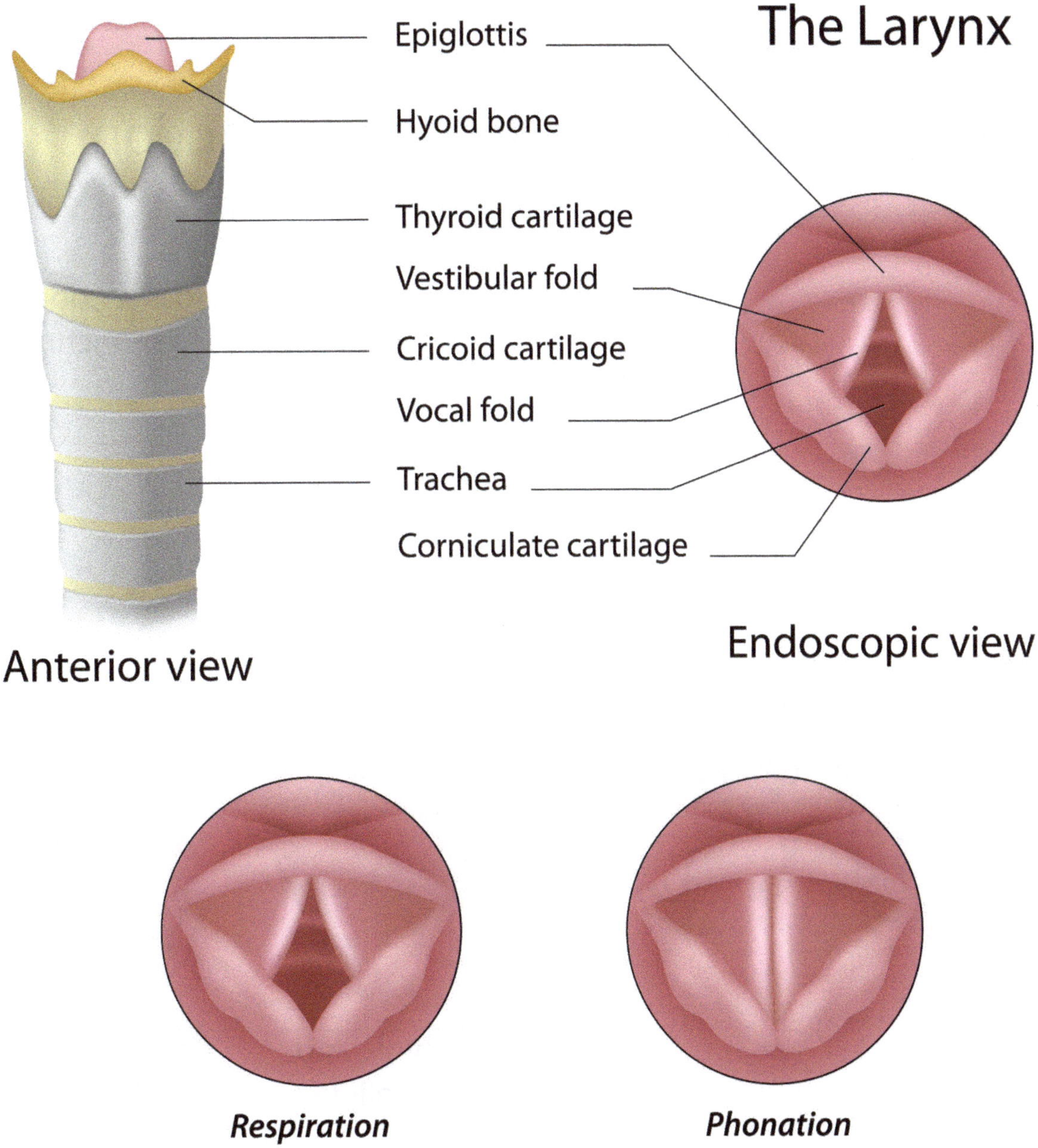

Epiglottis
Hyoid bone
Thyroid cartilage
Vestibular fold
Cricoid cartilage
Vocal fold
Trachea
Corniculate cartilage
Anterior view
Endoscopic view
Respiration
Phonation

# Human Lung Anatomy and Function

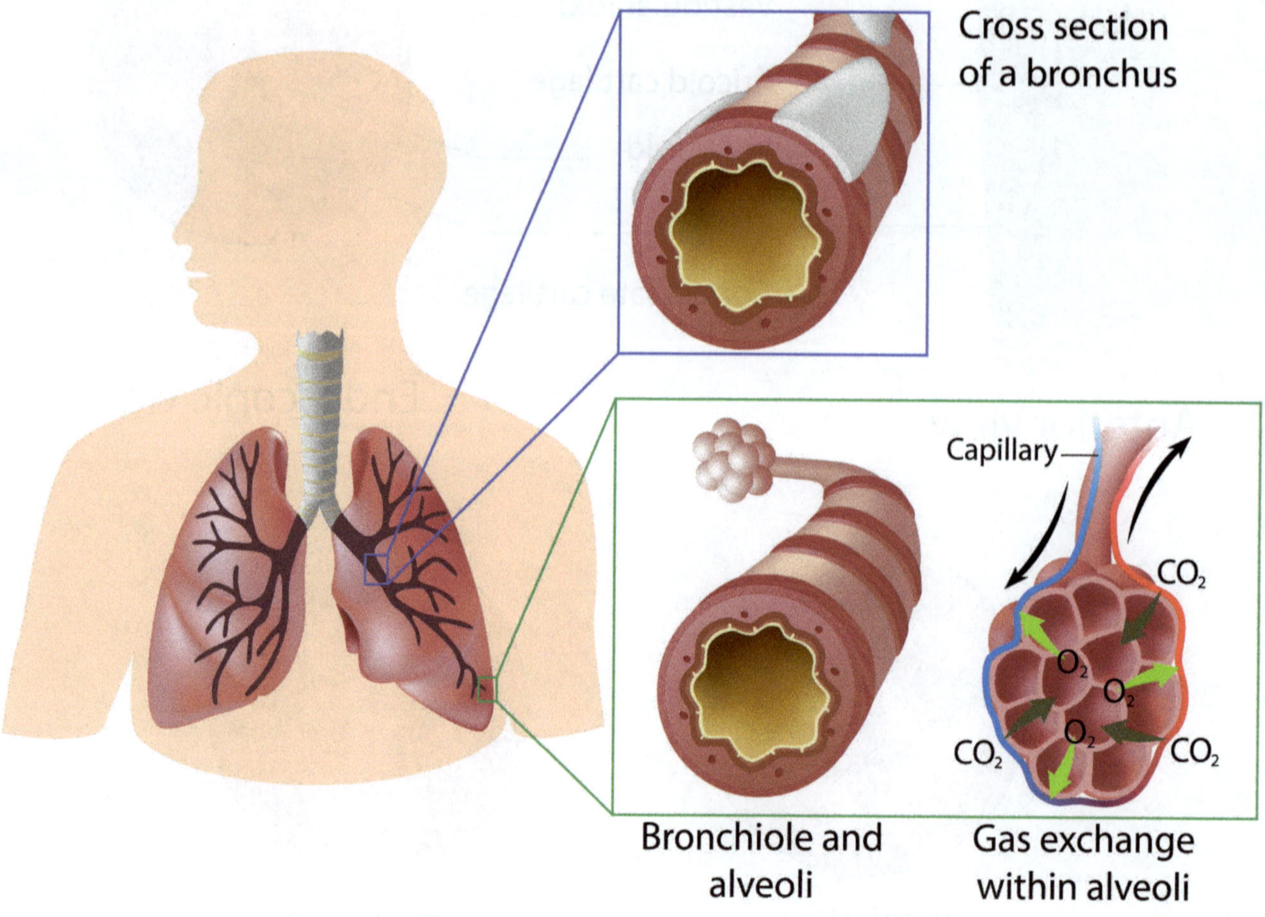

The lungs are a pair of large, spongy organs found in the thorax lateral to the heart and superior to the diaphragm. Each lung is surrounded by a pleural membrane that provides the lung with space to expand as well as a negative pressure space relative to the body's exterior. The negative pressure allows the lungs to passively fill with air as they relax.

# Digestive System

The digestive system is a group of organs working together to convert food into energy and basic nutrients to feed the entire body. Food passes through a long tube inside the body known as the alimentary canal or the gastrointestinal tract (GI tract). The alimentary canal is made up of the oral cavity, pharynx, esophagus, stomach, small intestines, and large intestines.

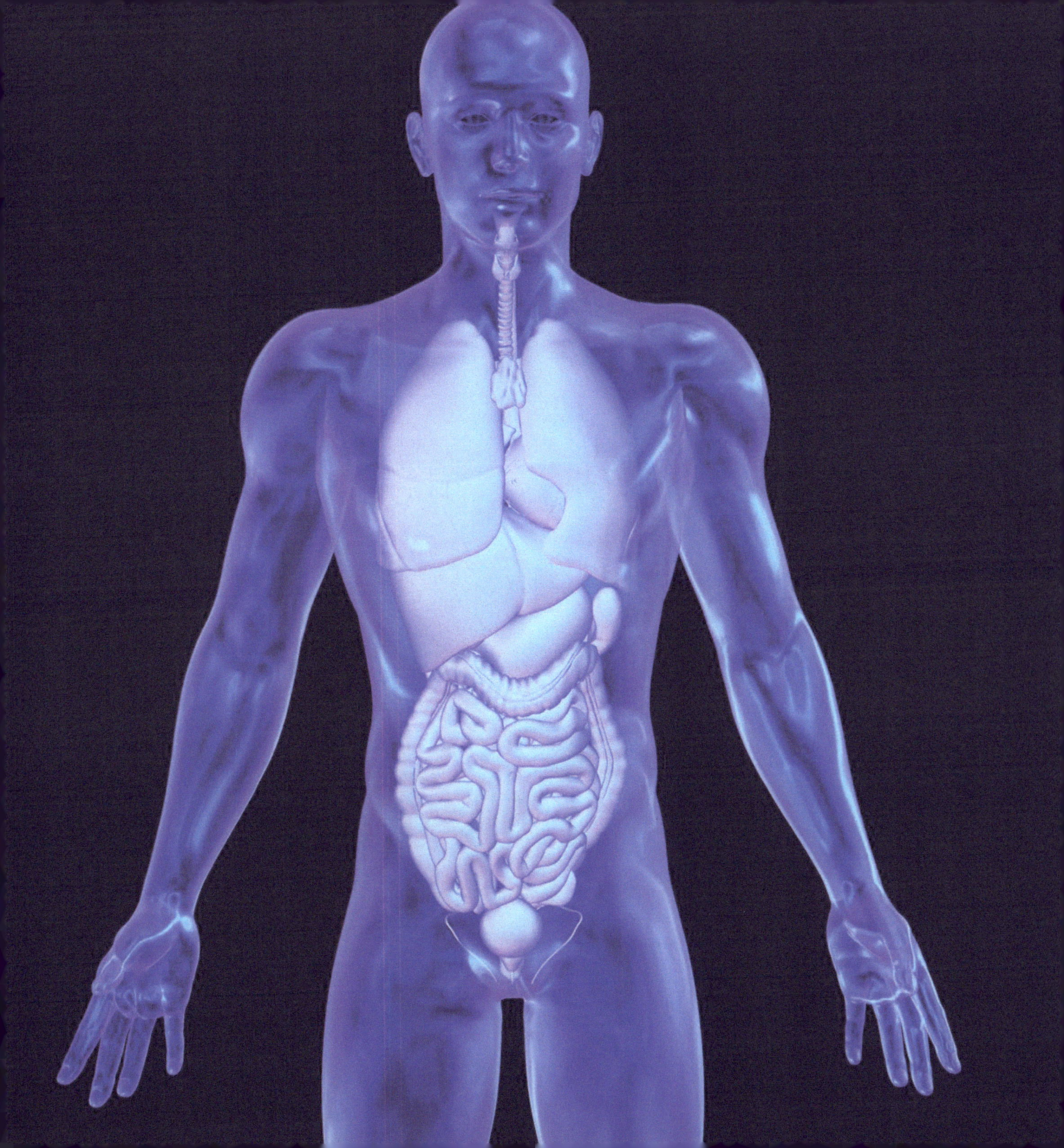

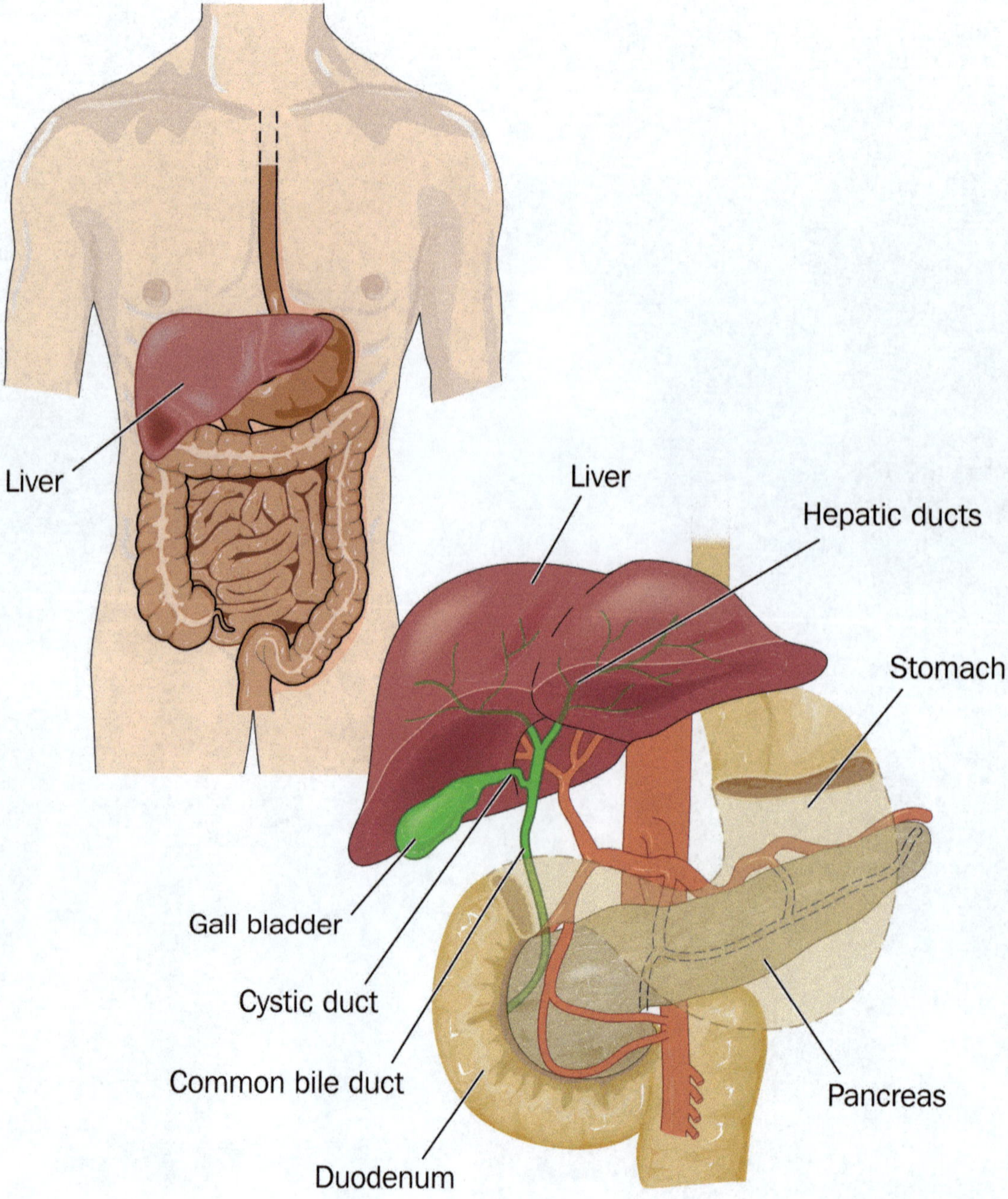
Liver
Liver
Hepatic ducts
Stomach
Gall bladder
Cystic duct
Common bile duct
Pancreas
Duodenum

The liver has many different functions in the body, but the main function of the liver in digestion is the production of bile and its secretion into the small intestine. The gallbladder is a small, pear-shaped organ located just posterior to the liver. The gallbladder is used to store and recycle excess bile from the small intestine so that it can be reused for the digestion of subsequent meals.

Food begins its journey through the digestive system in the mouth, also known as the oral cavity. Inside the mouth are many accessory organs that aid in the digestion of food—the tongue, teeth, and salivary glands. Teeth chop food into small pieces, which are moistened by saliva before the tongue and other muscles push the food into the pharynx.

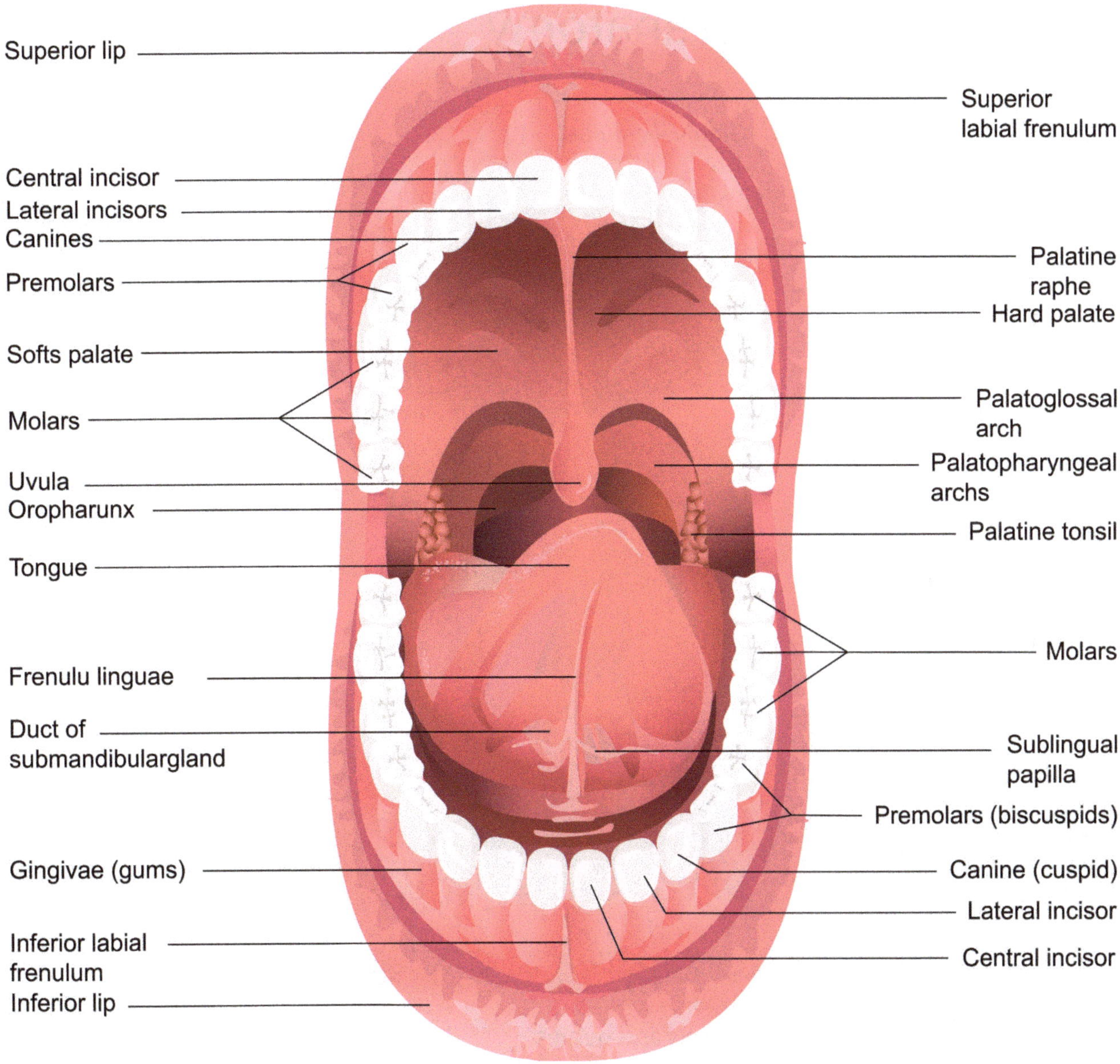
Superior lip
Superior labial frenulum
Central incisor
Lateral incisors
Canines
Premolars
Palatine raphe
Hard palate
Softs palate
Molars
Palatoglossal arch
Uvula
Oropharunx
Palatopharyngeal archs
Palatine tonsil
Tongue
Molars
Frenulu linguae
Duct of submandibulargland
Sublingual papilla
Premolars (biscuspids)
Gingivae (gums)
Canine (cuspid)
Lateral incisor
Inferior labial frenulum
Central incisor
Inferior lip

# Tooth anatomy

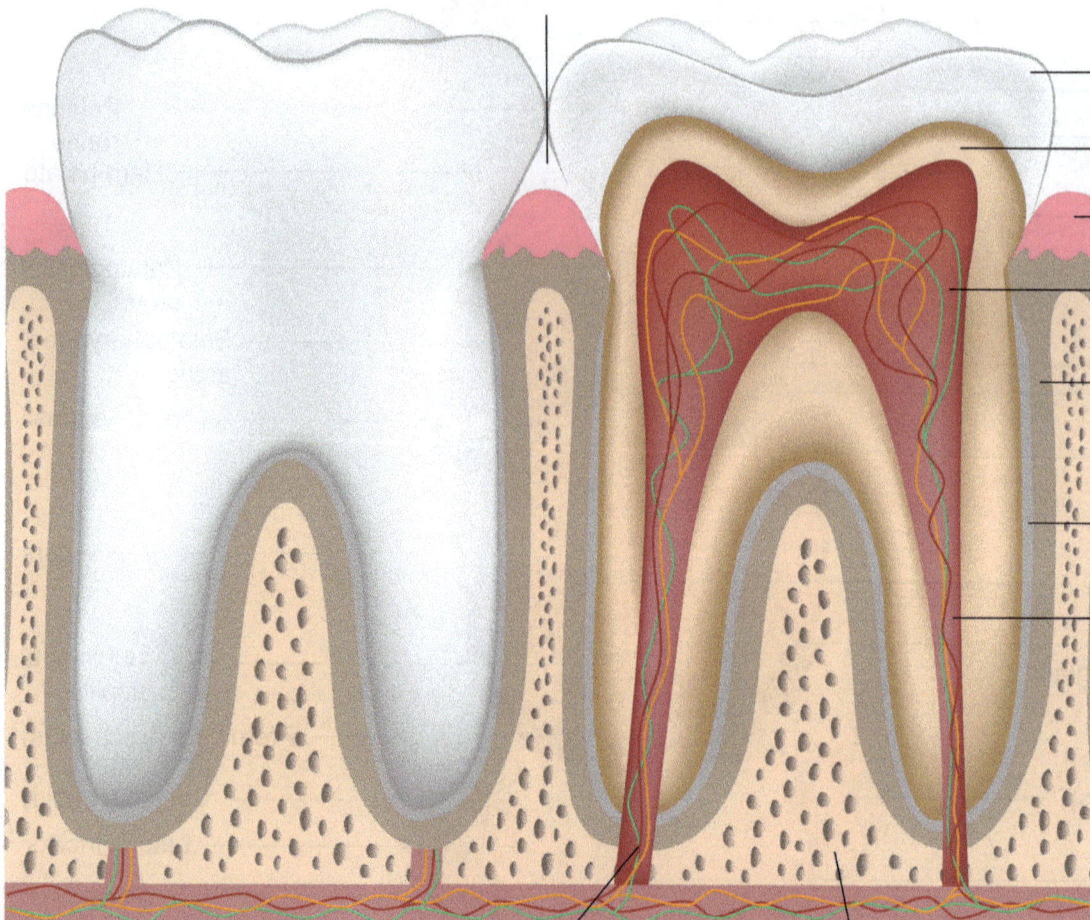

The teeth are 32 small, hard organs found along the anterior and lateral edges of the mouth. Each tooth is made of a bone-like substance called dentin and covered in a layer of enamel—the hardest substance in the body. The teeth are designed for cutting and grinding food into smaller pieces.

The stomach is a muscular sac that is located on the left side of the abdominal cavity, just inferior to the diaphragm. This major organ acts as a storage tank for food so that the body has time to digest large meals properly. The stomach also contains hydrochloric acid and digestive enzymes that continue the digestion of food that began in the mouth.

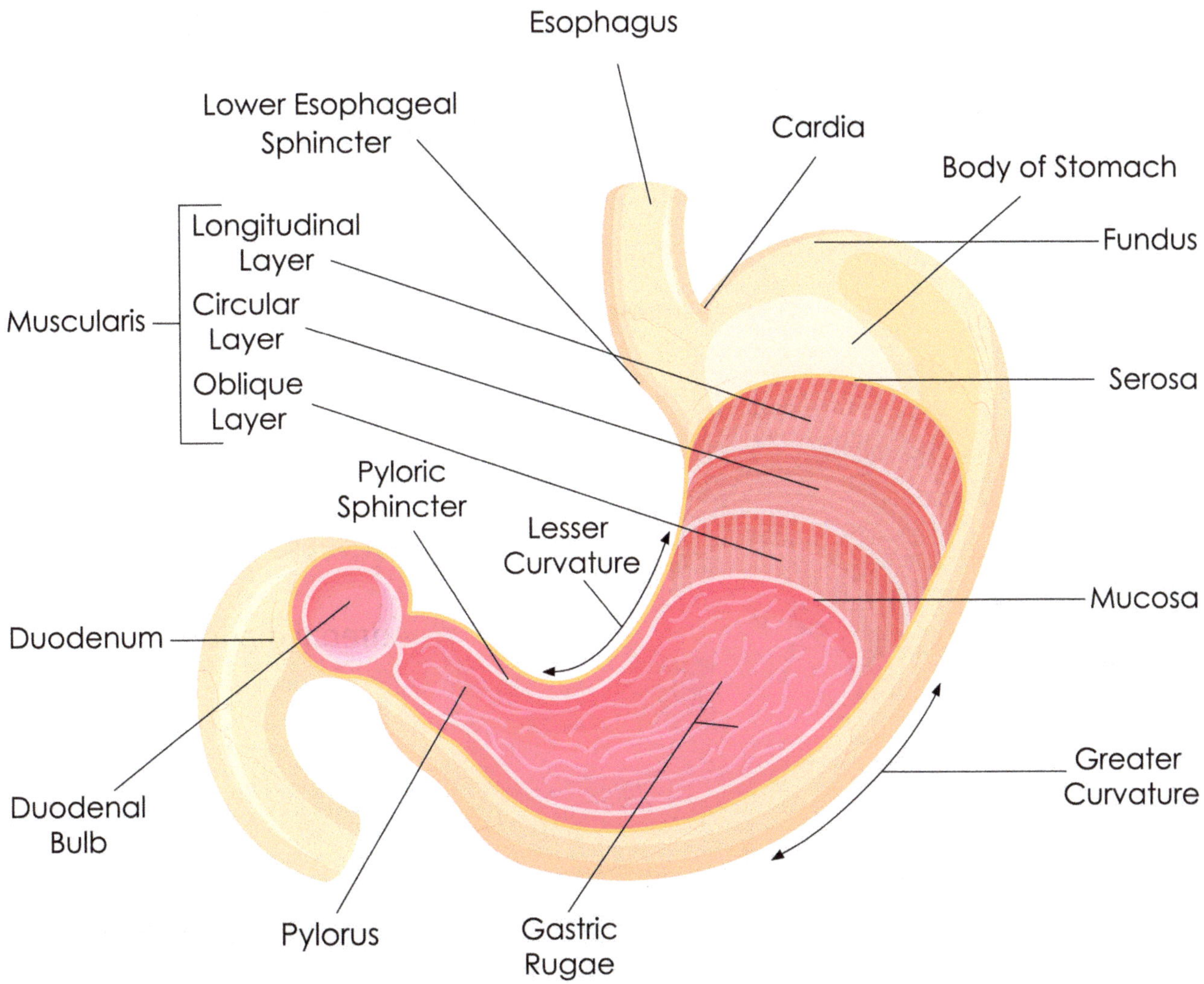
Esophagus
Lower Esophageal Sphincter
Cardia
Body of Stomach
Fundus
Longitudinal Layer
Circular Layer
Oblique Layer
Muscularis
Serosa
Pyloric Sphincter
Lesser Curvature
Mucosa
Duodenum
Duodenal Bulb
Greater Curvature
Pylorus
Gastric Rugae

# Stomach

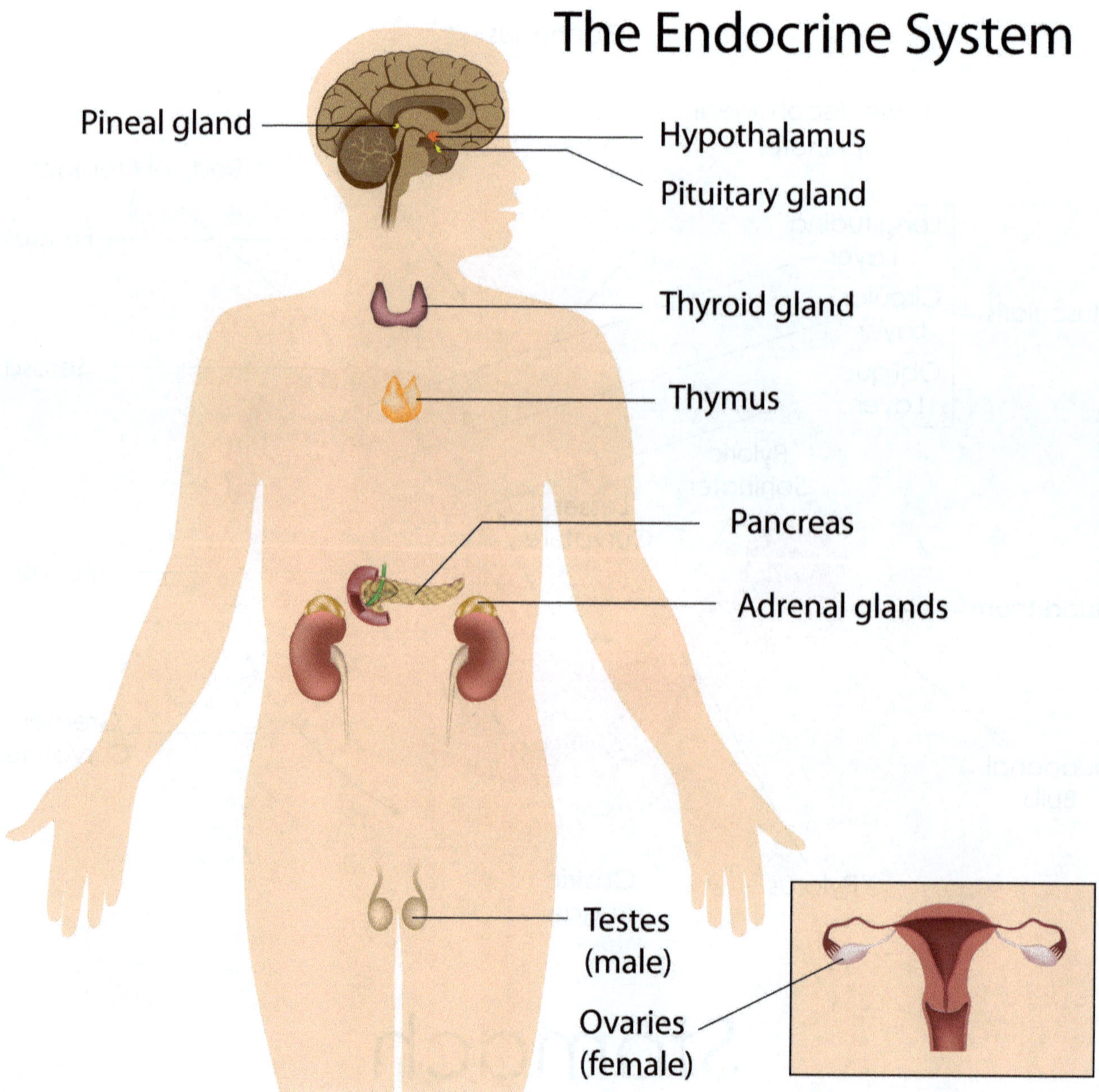
The Endocrine System
Pineal gland
Hypothalamus
Pituitary gland
Thyroid gland
Thymus
Pancreas
Adrenal glands
Testes
(male)
Ovaries
(female)

# Endocrine System

The endocrine system includes all of the glands of the body and the hormones produced by those glands. The glands are controlled directly by stimulation from the nervous system as well as by chemical receptors in the blood and hormones produced by other glands. By regulating the functions of organs in the body, these glands help to maintain the body's homeostasis.

The pituitary gland, also known as the hypophysis, is a small pea-sized lump of tissue connected to the inferior portion of the hypothalamus of the brain. Many blood vessels surround the pituitary gland to carry the hormones it releases throughout the body.

# The Pituitary Gland

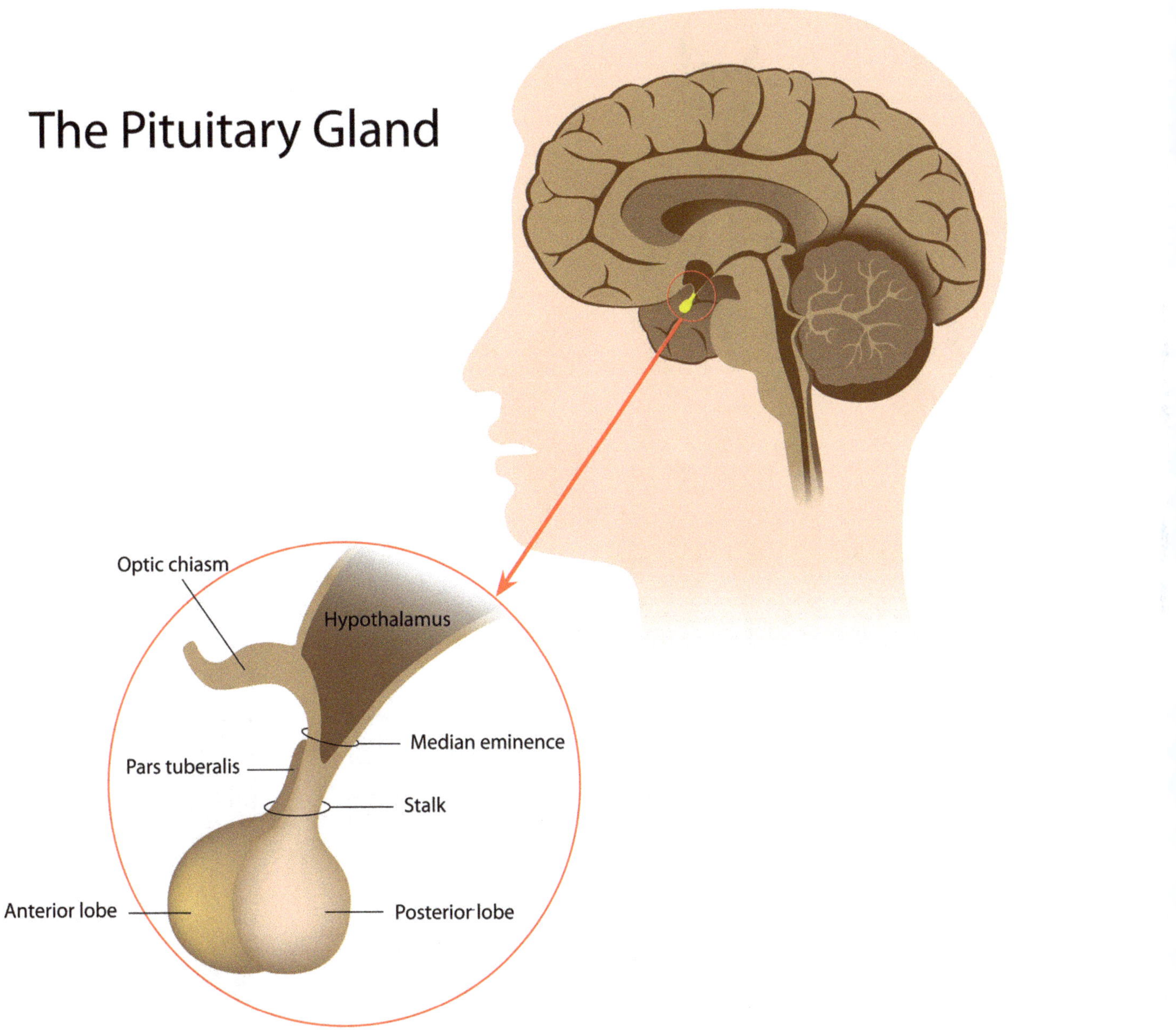

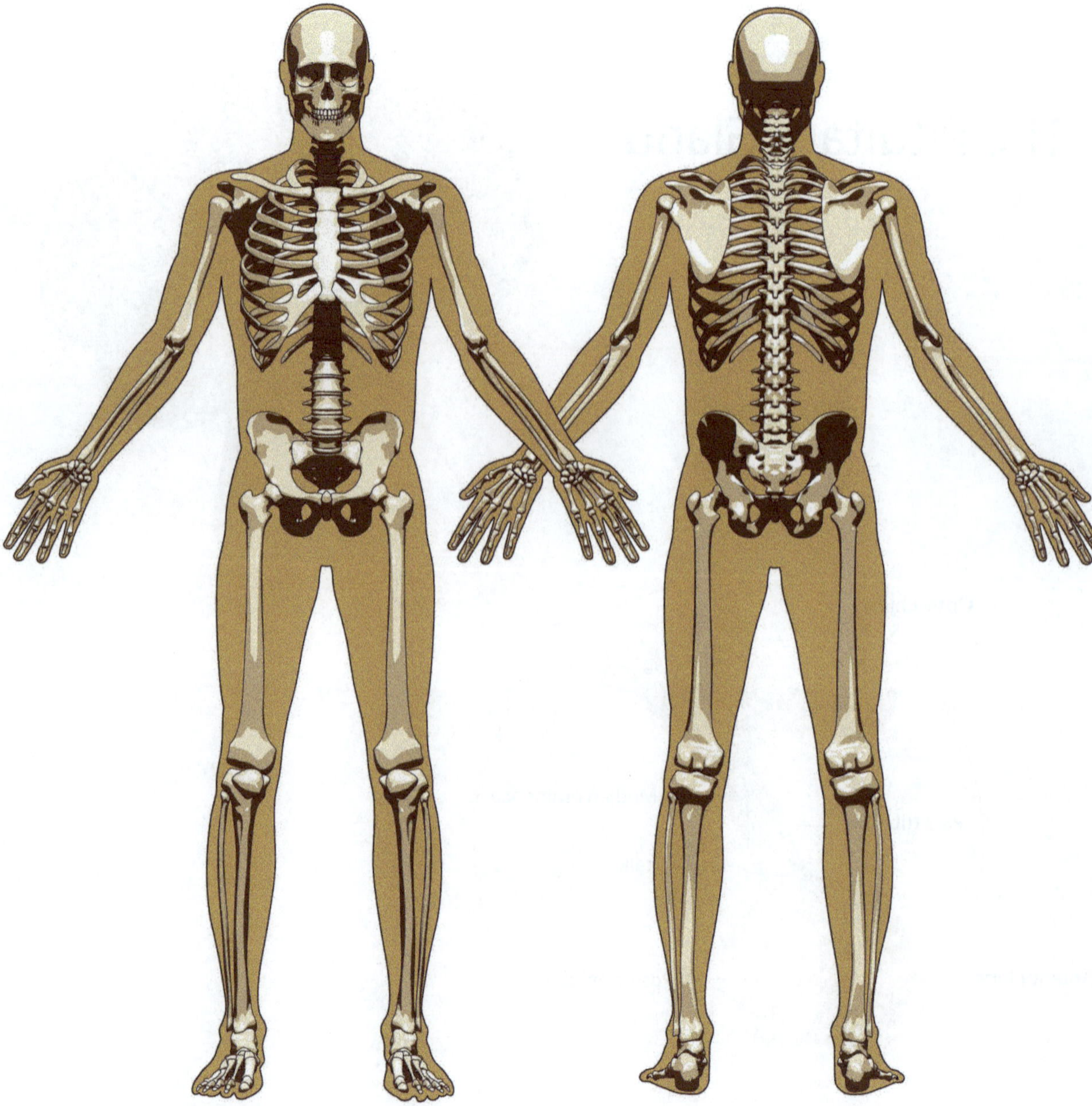

# Skeletal System

The skeletal system includes all of the bones and joints in the body. Each bone is a complex living organ that is made up of many cells, protein fibers, and minerals. The skeleton acts as a scaffold by providing support and protection for the soft tissues that make up the rest of the body. The skeletal system also provides attachment points for muscles to allow movements at the joints. New blood cells are produced by the red bone marrow inside of our bones.

The majority of human bones have a dense, strong outer layer, followed by a spongy part full of air for lightness, while the middle contains a soft, flexible, tissue substance called bone marrow. Calcium is very important for our bones and helps keep them strong and healthy.

# BONE ANATOMY

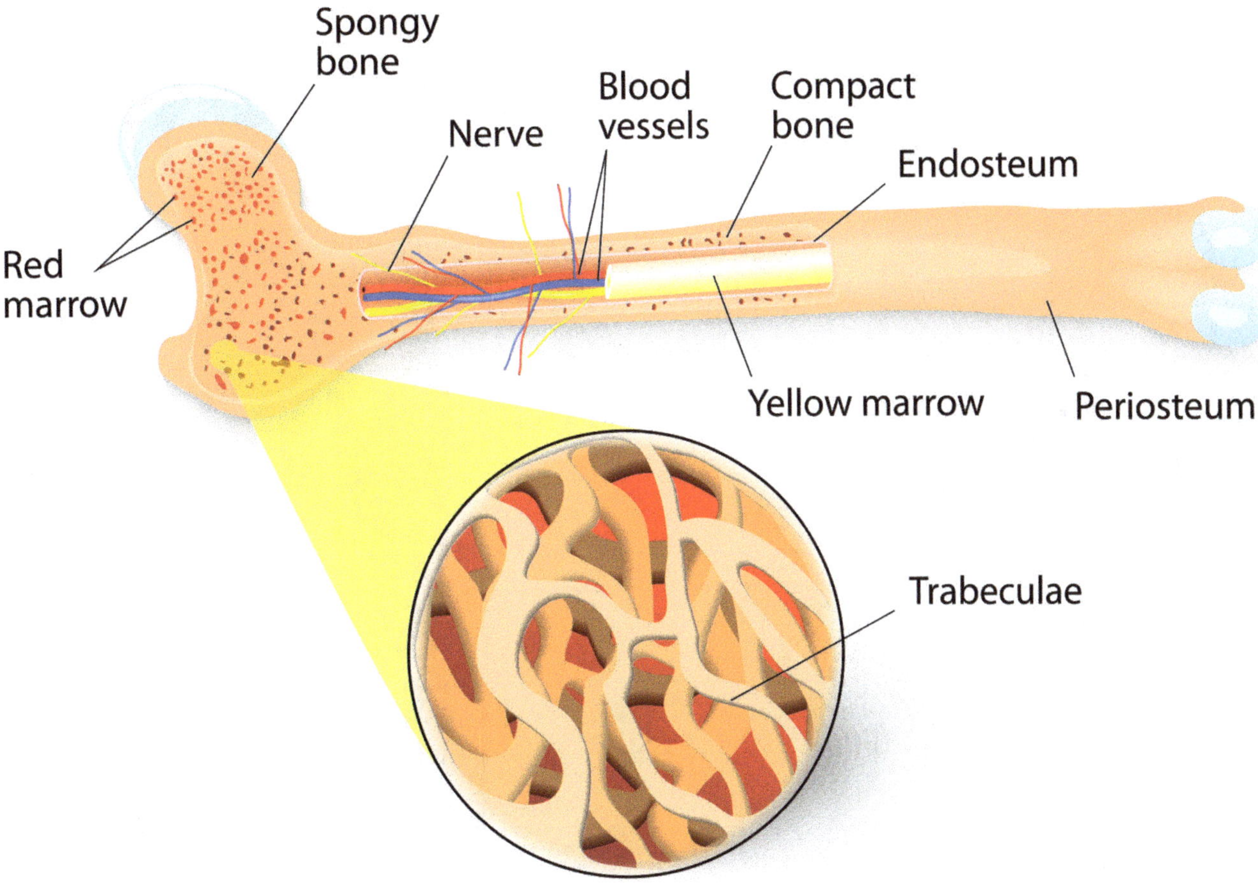

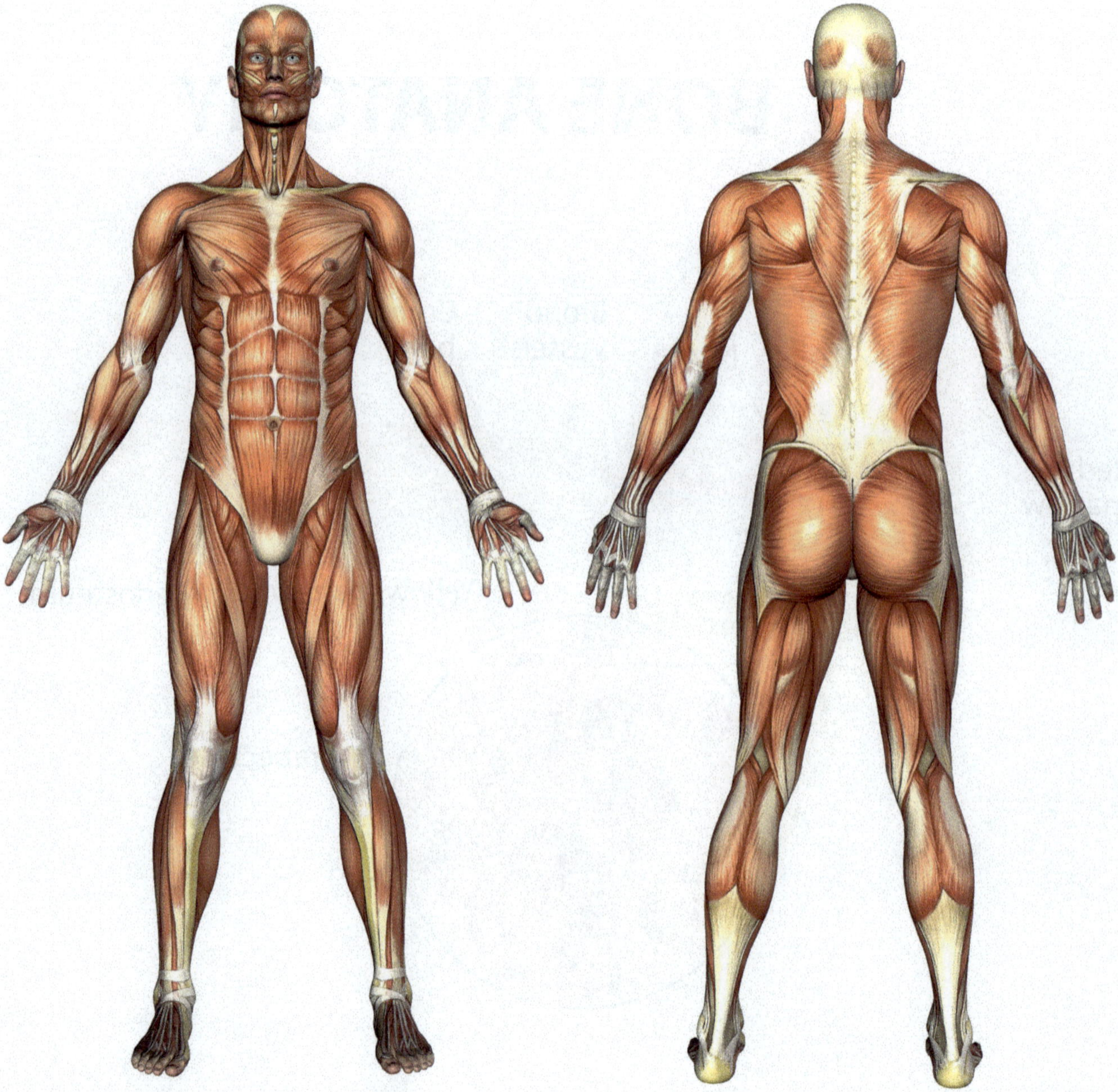

# Mascular System

The muscular system is responsible for the movement of the human body. Attached to the bones of the skeletal system are about 700 named muscles that make up roughly half of a person's body weight. Each of these muscles is a discrete organ constructed of skeletal muscle tissue, blood vessels, tendons, and nerves. Muscle tissue is also found inside of the heart, digestive organs, and blood vessels.

Skeletal muscle is the only voluntary muscle tissue in the human body—it is controlled consciously. Every physical action that a person consciously performs (e.g. speaking, walking, or writing) requires skeletal muscle. The function of skeletal muscle is to contract to move parts of the body closer to the bone that the muscle is attached to. Most skeletal muscles are attached to two bones across a joint, so the muscle serves to move parts of those bones closer to each other.

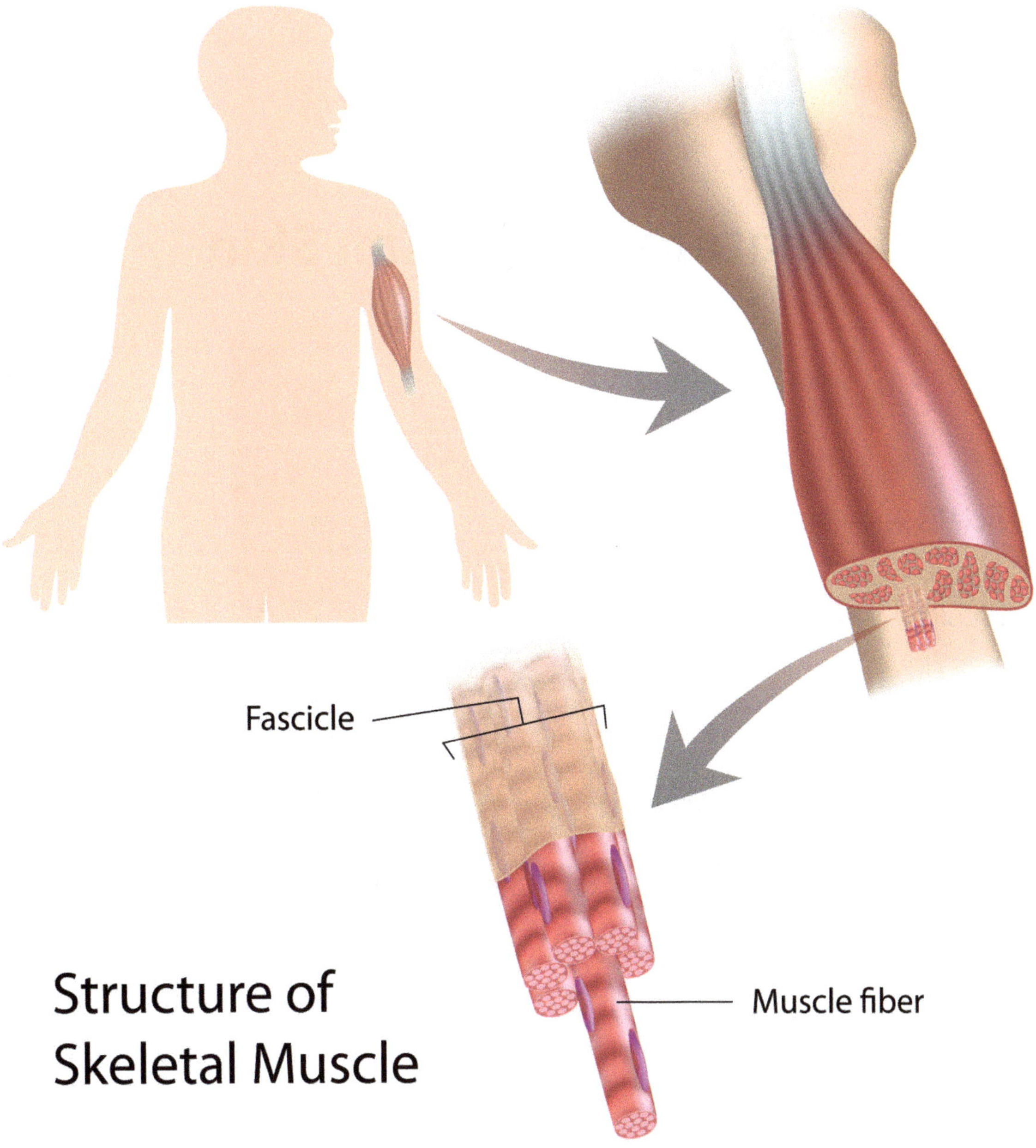
Fascicle
Muscle fiber
Structure of
Skeletal Muscle

# Anatomy of Human Skin

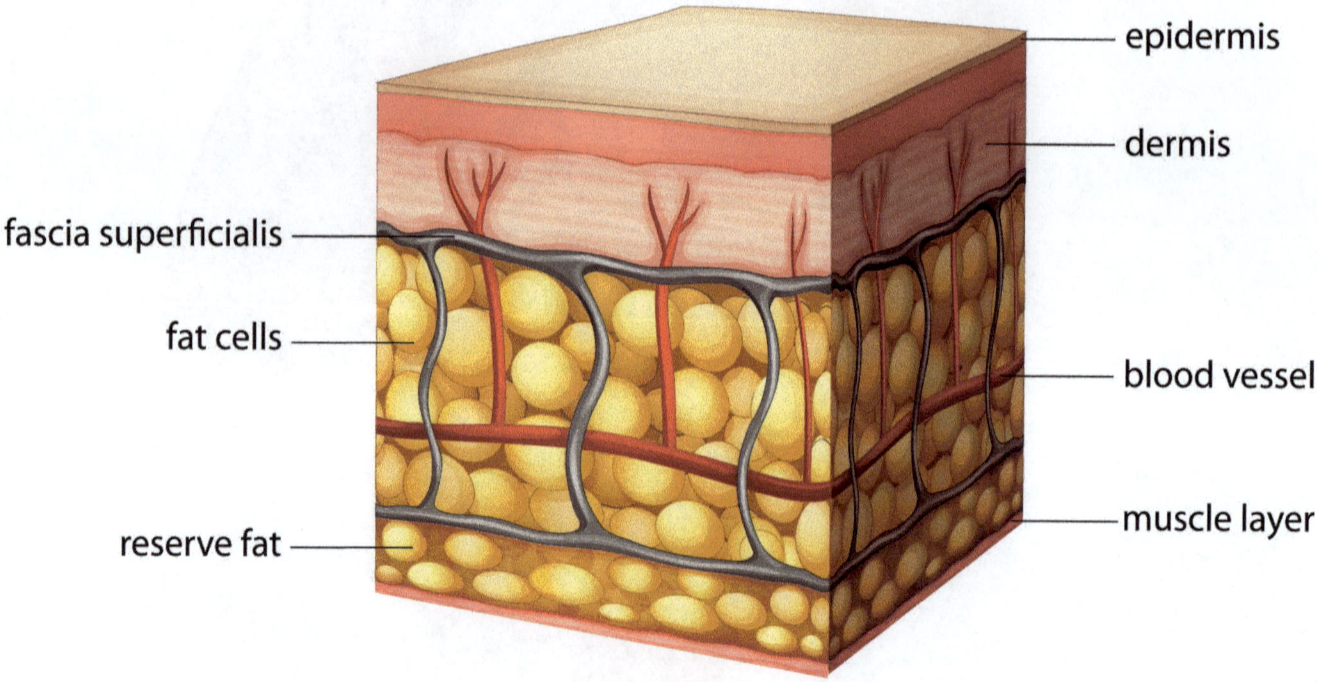

# IntegumentarySystem

The integumentary system is an organ system consisting of the skin, hair, nails, and exocrine glands. The skin is only a few millimeters thick yet is by far the largest organ in the body. Skin forms the body's outer covering and forms a barrier to protect the body from chemicals, disease, UV light, and physical damage. Hair and nails extend from the skin to reinforce the skin and protect it from environmental damage.

Hair is an accessory organ of the skin made of columns of tightly packed dead keratinocytes found in most regions of the body. Hair helps to protect the body from UV radiation by preventing sunlight from striking the skin. Hair also insulates the body by trapping warm air around the skin.

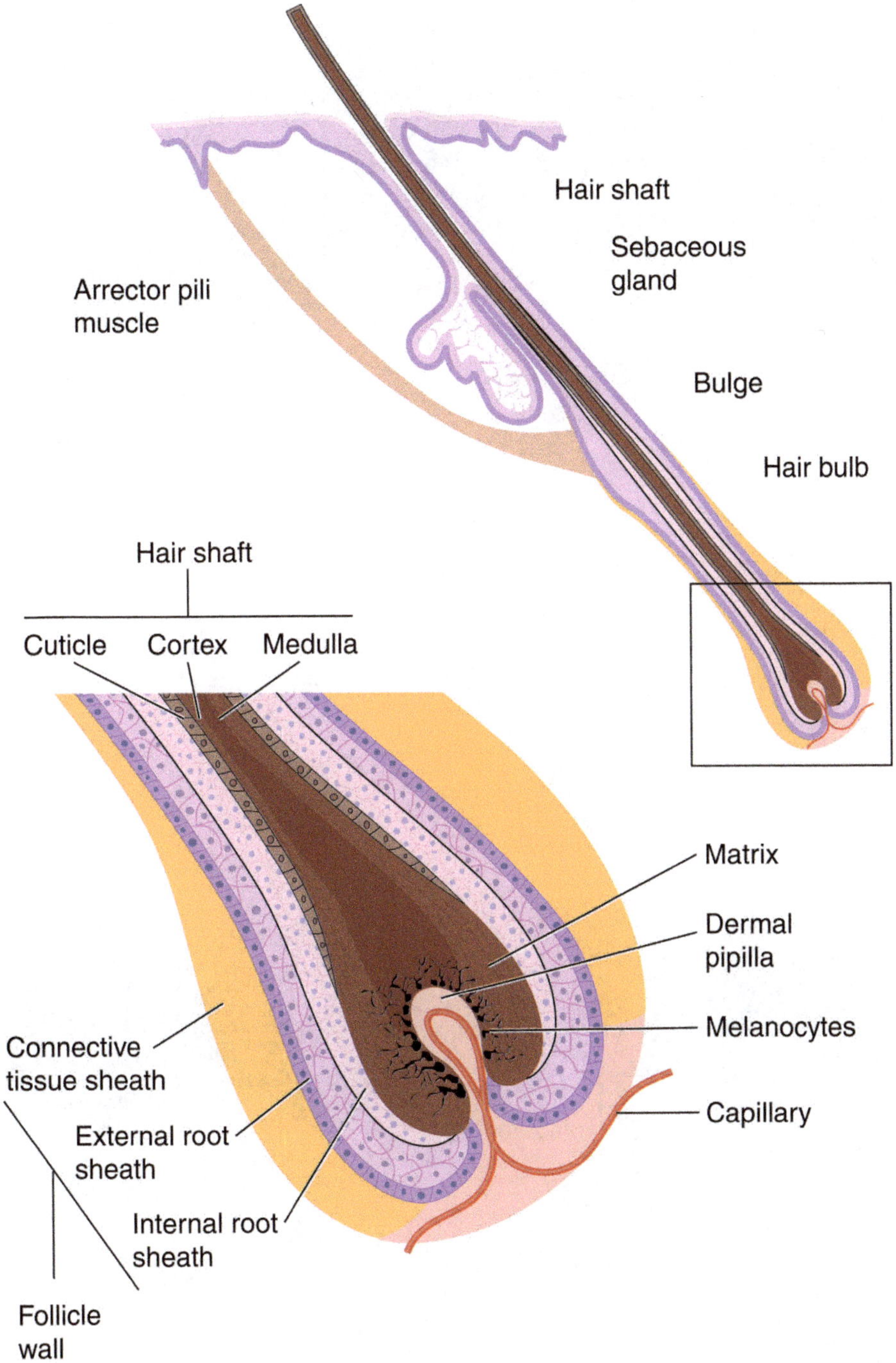
Hair shaft
Sebaceous gland
Arrector pili muscle
Bulge
Hair bulb
Hair shaft
Cuticle
Cortex
Medulla
Matrix
Dermal pipilla
Melanocytes
Capillary
Connective tissue sheath
External root sheath
Internal root sheath
Follicle wall

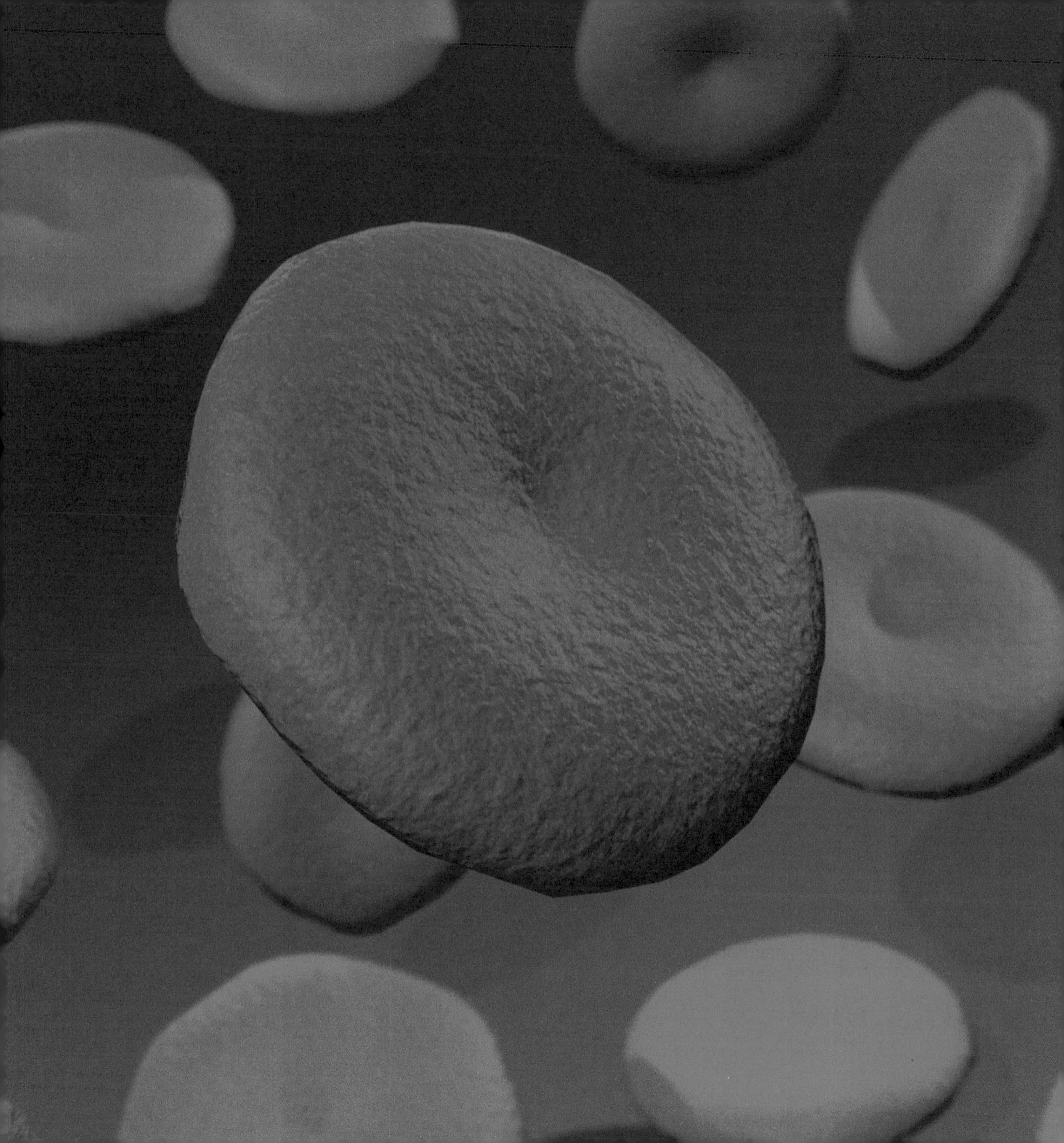

# Blood Cells

**The average human body contains about 4 to 5 liters of blood. As a liquid connective tissue, it transports many substances through the body and helps to maintain homeostasis of nutrients, wastes, and gases. Blood is made up of red blood cells, white blood cells, platelets, and liquid plasma.**

Lightning Source UK Ltd.
Milton Keynes UK
UKHW052216150919
349830UK00007B/262/P

9 781681 275536